"Gals!"
Girls As Leaders

by

Christine "Kris" Brumfield

To: Sonya!
Always Remember
the Sky is the Limit!
Christine Brumfield
9/07

AuthorHouse™
1663 Liberty Drive, Suite 200
Bloomington, IN 47403
www.authorhouse.com
Phone: 1-800-839-8640

AuthorHouse™ UK Ltd.
500 Avebury Boulevard
Central Milton Keynes, MK9 2BE
www.authorhouse.co.uk
Phone: 08001974150

First published by AuthorHouse 7/9/2007

ISBN: 978-1-4259-2775-2 (sc)

Printed in the United States of America
Bloomington, Indiana

This book is printed on acid-free paper.

Front Cover Artwork / Illustration by Elaine Young – Hopscotch Communications, Dallas, Texas.

Front and Back Cover Design by Cathi Stevenson – Book Cover Express, Nova Scotia – Canada.

Bloomington, IN Milton Keynes, UK

authorHOUSE®

GALS!™
Girls As Leaders!™

****

****

Inspiring Words of Encouragement, Maxims, & Paraphrases
For You to Reach Out,
Follow Your Passion in Life,
Motivate, & Inspire

Most of all, this book will inspire you to

"Dare to Dream"
&
"Believe"
&
"Reach For the Stars"

****

****

Dedication

A very special remembrance and thanks to my mom, Lucille, who shared with me the gift of tolerance and patience with children.

Even though it's been said that the sky is the limit, we must remember that our possibilities are limitless.

Introduction!

****

This book has been designed as a resource to meet the needs of many different viewers, from young girls in their early years to young ladies ready for the world. It was written with the sincere passion to share with young girls and young ladies the fact that what they do in life becomes the foundation that will ultimately define who they are or can become.

The common goal amongst the range of young girls to young ladies is the encouragement for each of them to pursue their dreams.

My hope is that I offer a great resource that respects the diversity and character of all young girls and young ladies and will be engaged on all levels.

Girls need to know they can find inspiration in many of their everyday surroundings and they can also be an inspiration to others. This is the reason why I felt inspired to share the importance of believing in your dreams, having great character and core values, controlling your emotions, and being a great leader, and how that will help them to grow and be productive citizens.

This book shares inspiring maxims, words of wisdom, and paraphrases that provide the guidance you will need in order to reach for the stars, believe in yourself, and follow your passion in life.

I know that girls can be great leaders in so many ways and the name GALS! – Girls As Leaders! was created to guide and inspire you to be all you can.

You must remember, "No one can make you feel inferior without your consent."
  • – Eleanor Roosevelt

Traditional English Prayer

Take time to work — it is the price of success.

Take time to think — it is the source of power.

Take time to play — it is the secret of perpetual youth.

Take time to read — it is the foundation of wisdom.

Take time to be friendly — it is the road to happiness.

Take time to dream — it is hitching your wagon to a star.

Take time to love and be loved — it is the privilege of God.

Take time to look around — it is too short a day to be selfish.

Take time to laugh — it is the music of the soul.

DARE to DREAM

Table of Contents!

****

Dare to Dream!

****

You know… GALS!™ – Girls As Leaders!™ can do anything.

Follow your dreams, listen to your heart, and let your dreams, character, core values, emotions, and **leadership** skills be your reward to life's pleasures.

> "Dreams are the touchstones of our character."
>
> • –Henry David Thoreau,
> (1817–1862) American author

> "The future belongs to those who believe in the beauty of their dreams."
>
> • – Eleanor Roosevelt

Chapter 1

Dare to Dream!

****

Within this inspiring chapter, entitled "Dare to Dream", take note of the maxims, quotations, paraphrases, and short, meaningful paragraphs for you to embrace and take to heart.

"Dreams are what get you started. Discipline is what keeps you going."

- • – Jim Ryun

Having discipline helps you to maintain a sense of balance in your everyday life. There will always be challenges and opportunities in your life that will inspire and guide you in many directions. As you make decisions, remember that they will reflect on who you are as an individual.

As you grow from young girls into young ladies and finally into thriving adults, remember that you are defining who you really are along the way, so you must choose your decisions wisely.

We are often conditioned to think that our lives revolve around great moments. Great moments often catch us unaware, beautifully wrapped in what others may consider a small one. Always be proud of who you are.

You must keep in mind, "People will forget what you did, but people will never forget how you made them feel."

- • – Maya Angelou

It's okay to make mistakes along the way, but at some point in your life, as you dare to dream you will find passion and energy which will drive the strength from within your very soul to be different and you should not feel any shame about the choices you make, or the paths you decide to take. Remember, it's your life, it's your journey.

Chapter 1

Dare to Dream!

****

"It's better to be hated for what you are than to be loved for something you are not."

• – Andre Gide

As you go through life, you should follow those mental thoughts and dreams that challenge you to be different – believe, dream, embrace life, and put it all in the hands of God. Trust and listen to your inner voice.

Let your thoughts and dreams flow endlessly and do something positive with them.

"The best and most beautiful things in the world cannot be seen or even touched. They must be felt with the heart."

• – Helen Keller

Always remember that you are unique. Not like everyone else. Keep an open mind and know that there is good in everyone, you just have to look for it.

"If you can change your mind, you can change your life."

• – William James

"What is popular is not always right, and what is right is not always popular." Don't be afraid to be different.

• – Unknown

Watch your thoughts; they become your actions. Watch your actions; they become your habits. Watch your habits; they become your character; Watch your character; it becomes your destiny.

"Blessed are those who can give without remembering and take without forgetting."

• – Elizabeth Bibesco

Dare to Dream!

****

Some of us see things as they are and say "Why?", you have the internal power to dare to dream things that never were and say, "Why Not?"

No one else can fulfill your dreams. Stay focused, protect your dreams and maintain a healthy optimistic attitude.

Look to this day. Yesterday is but a dream, and tomorrow is only a vision. But today, if well-lived, makes every yesterday a dream of happiness and every tomorrow a vision of hope.

"Change and growth take place when a person has risked himself and dares to become involved with experimenting with his own life."

• – Herbert Otto

"Daring ideas are like chessmen moved forward; they may be beaten, but they may start a winning game."

• – Goethe

GALS!™ know that persistence, enthusiasm, and planning will help guide you to success.

A woman once said to the great violinist Fritz Kreisler after a recital, "I'd give my life to play as beautifully as you!" Madam Kreisler replied, "I have."

"I tell them that if you stay committed, your dreams can come true. I'm living proof of it. I left home at seventeen and had nothing but rejections for twenty-five years. I wrote more than twenty screenplays, but I never gave up."

• – Michael Blake, author of Dances with Wolves

Dare to Dream!

****

"The greatest pleasure in life is doing what people say can't be done."

- – From an advertisement by Northern Trust Business Banking

"The soul never thinks without a picture."

- – Aristotle

As we live out our dreams, we must keep certain values that are important to us.

Those values, which are known as core values, help define who you are as individuals.

Core values, are a combination of definitive character traits, beliefs, and moral standards that help define and nurture us towards individuality.

"Leave nothing for tomorrow which can be done today."

- – Abraham Lincoln, 16th U.S. President (1809 - 1865)

GALs!™, you should always behave in ways that make you feel good about who you are.

Character is all about being you and staying the course, never allowing anyone to define you except yourself. It is okay to seek out role models, but you must first understand who you are.

"Making time for your dreams is not selfish. Some people with passion and dreams actually live longer, healthier lives. It is often an act of generosity to make time for your dreams that make you happy."

- – Marcia Wieder

Dare to Dream!

****

To get you started, make yourself a dream board, adding pictures, inspirational thoughts, and fun items to get your creative dreaming started each day.

Your dreams offer a tremendous opportunity for you to create a huge amount of ideas that could influence your daily life with creativity.

As you read each chapter dream vividly. Write down your thoughts. Think about yourself in many situations, in different places and surroundings, with different friends and family members, and with different cultures.

Embrace the following chapter on character and core values, for it is filled with inspiring information and resources for you to use in your everyday life. Cherish it!

"There is a world of experiences awaiting us, if we take the time to take them. Age does not determine what we know."

- – Rosa Parks, civil rights leader (1913 – 2005)

"Dare to Dream!"

Character & Core Values!

****

GALS!™, do you know if you have good character and core values? Do you have a good understanding of what the words mean? Take to heart this chapter and find out.

Your character is a combination of the core values. Let's first understand the two concepts.

Core values, include responsibility, ethics, courage, trustworthiness, integrity, fairness, teamwork, passion, honesty, citizenship, excellence, diversity, caring, trust, service, empathy, diligence, and respect.

Character is the way you really are. It's the way you act even when no one is looking. Good people do good deeds not for show, not for credit or adulation, but just as an expression of their true spirit. These are the people who we say have good character.

Most people say they want to be good, but developing good character takes more than words.

Good people are people of action---they take care of themselves and others.

They can be depended upon to do the right thing, even when the right thing is the hardest thing to do. One of the things they do is behave responsively.

The importance of character and core values in our lives is so important that this next section is divided into three subsections that, when combined, will inspire you to become citizens of great character.

The first section is called the Six C's of Character, developed by Michael Josephson, president and founder of the Josephson Institute and Character Counts! The second section is called the Virtues, and the last section is called Eight Strengths of Character, and was developed by Thomas Lickona.

Character & Core Values!

****

This powerful combination is the ultimate in embracing and engaging the importance of having great character. This combination also provides a well-rounded recipe for developing great character.

– Six C's of Character –

The Six C's of Character says, "the best road to a better life is to be a better person, and all of us can be better."

One of the best ways to do this is to focus on the Six C's of Character: conscience, courage, consideration, compassion, confidence and control.

The first C is Conscience. GALS!™, you should listen to the inner voice that helps you know right from wrong and urges you to do what is good and noble.

The second C is Courageous. GALS!™, you should resolve to confront the challenges and choices of your life in a way that will make you proud of your decisions. Make the tough decisions that need to be made and, above all, maintain your integrity by doing what you know to be right, even when it costs more than what you are willing to pay.

The third C is Considerate. GALS!™, you should be more deliberate, thoughtful, and attentive as to how your words and actions will affect others and reflect on your character. Think ahead so you can avoid undesirable and undesired consequences.

The Six C's of Character were identified by Michael Josephson in his Free Weekly Commentary E-Newsletter #443 (Dec. 30, 2005 – Jan. 5, 2006) and used with permission of the Josephson Institute of Ethics, ©2006 www.charactercounts.org. All rights reserved.

Character & Core Values!

****

The fourth C is Compassionate. GALS!™, you should demonstrate a genuine concern for the well-being of others. Be kinder and more charitable. Strive to understand more and judge less.

The fifth C is Confident. GALS!™, you should be confident in your capacity to overcome with integrity and dignity whatever difficulties come your way.

You should not under estimate your resiliency. Be persistent until you prevail.

The sixth C is Control. GALS!™, you should control any strong emotions, appetites and urges that tempt you to compromise your principles or sacrifice long-term goals for short-term indulgences.

Remember, your character is your destiny. Begin with the end in mind.

– The Virtues –

When we behave responsibly we should always maintain a strong sense of character, which consists of the virtues that are important for strong character.

There are over one hundred virtues, which can be divided into moral or performance virtues. They can be thought of as bringing out the best in ourselves and others at home, in the classroom, and in your community. Essentially helping you to become the best you can be.

Character & Core Values!

****

Virtues can be described as the essence of the human spirit and the content of our character. What are some of the virtues for strong character?   A few are listed below.

Love	Humility	Tolerance	Integrity
Wisdom	Self-discipline	Justice	Loyalty
Kindness	Caring	Unity	Honor
Understanding	Courtesy		Obedience
Patience	Honesty	Diligence	Courage
Compassion	Courage	Perseverance	Respect
Forgiveness	Gratitude	Confidence	

You can inspire others and be inspired by the language of virtue.

Each one of the virtues can create a culture of character that you can use to evaluate your performance.

Think about selecting one of the virtues to focus on for a full week and see how you personally can use that virtue in your life.

The virtues are to inspire all GALS!™, to discover that this compilation of values, are inherent within each of them.

Character & Core Values!

✳✳

As you select a virtue, think how that particular virtue can help you to cultivate strengths or improve upon weaknesses that you think you may have, and pursue a goal. Learn to challenge life, take risks.

Recognize that the virtues can help you become outstanding GALS!™, of character, the person you dream of being, that beautiful person that you are.

The virtues are like shining stars that twinkle with enlightened power, that will inspire, lead, and brighten your faith with one of the greatest gifts in life, your character.

As you dream the impossible and lead with that shining star twinkling within, use the virtues to:

- Believe in yourself
- Follow your dreams
- Be the inspiration in someone's life
- Share your stories
- Confront your greatest challenge

What we know for sure, is that the greatest fire is often started from a single flame…for each of you, the choices you make, the core values that each of you possess, the character you have and the virtues you cherish the most --- are priceless.

GALS!™, as you do the right thing, know that the virtues will play a great part in shaping your life.

Character & Core Values!

****

In life, when you set goals, and have plans, often times you will reach a milestone or even a road block. Accept the challenge to move forward and believe that you are capable of reaching for the stars and know that your possibilities are endless.

The virtues prized in free countries are honesty, self-discipline, a sense of responsibility to one's family, a sense of loyalty to ones employer and staff, and a pride in the quality of one's work. These virtues only flourish in a climate of freedom.
- – Margaret Thatcher

The virtues are a guide that will inspire you to be:

- V … Virtuous
- I … Inspirational
- R … Reliable
- T … Trustworthy
- U … Understanding
- E … Exciting

"Follow your instincts, that's where true wisdom will manifest itself."
- – Oprah Winfrey

Acting with integrity can be thought as of bringing our virtues and values into alignment. While virtue requires belief and acceptance; values requires commitment and action. While some consider virtue and value to be synonymous, one can accept the concept of virtuous behavior without necessarily valuing it.

Character & Core Values!

****

In this next section, I will share with you a few of the core values which are really important for you to have. They are responsibility, caring, fairness, trustworthiness, respect, and citizenship. This does not mean that the other core values are less important, but this set provides a foundation for you to start on a path of developing your ideas and inspirations as you dare to dream.

– Responsibility –

Responsible people do good things and do not take credit for other people's work, and they admit their own mistakes. They show self-control by choosing words or actions carefully. This means they think carefully before they say or do anything.

GALS!™, you can do your part by helping your families, teachers, neighbors, and friends, by trying your hardest and doing your best in everything you do.

As you think about your character and the responsibility that comes with it, there are core values that play a vital role in helping you shape those values. A responsible person will follow the Do's of responsibility:

– Responsibility Do's –

- Show you care about others through kindness, caring, generosity, and compassion.
- Think before you talk.
- Do only good things.
- Think about what will happen if you say or do what you want to say or do.
- Fix your mistakes. Clean up your own messes.

Character & Core Values!

****

- Be a good example.

- Do your job.

- Do your best and always keep trying.

- In terms of duty, acknowledge and meet your legal and moral obligations.

- In terms of accountability, you should accept responsibility for the consequences of your choices, not only for what you do but for what you don't do. You should think about your consequences on yourself and others before you act. Think long–term. Do what you can do to make things better. Always set a good example.

- In the pursuit of excellence, do your best, persevere, always be prepared, be diligent, work hard, and make all you do worthy of pride.

- In terms of self–control, take charge of your own life, set realistic goals, and keep a positive outlook. Be prudent and self-disciplined with your health, emotions, time, and money. You should be rational and act out of reason, not anger, revenge, or fear. Know the difference between what you have a right to do and what is right to do. Be self–reliant; manage your life so you are not dependent on others. Pay your own way whenever you can. Be independent.

– Responsibility Don'ts –

- Don't say anything before you think.

- Don't do anything that's wrong.

Character & Core Values!

****

- Don't blame others for your mistakes.
- Don't leave mistakes or messes for someone else to fix.
- Don't wait for someone to tell you to do good things.
- Don't do anything that you would not be proud of.
- Don't pretend to have done jobs you really haven't done.
- Don't look the other way when you can make a difference.

– Caring –

As we consider the core value word caring, we can see how it is just as important as the core value words responsibility, fairness, trustworthiness, respect, and citizenship.

A caring person is a bright spot in a sometimes grim world where crime, anger, fear, hunger, and loneliness have pushed even well-meaning people into isolation.

Caring is at the heart of an ethical person's character. It's a guideline for how an ethical person relates to the world and its people.

A caring person is considerate, kind, compassionate, and generous. A caring person always takes into account how decisions, words, and actions are likely to affect other people.

Character & Core Values!

****

GALs!™ may ask, "Why do people show consideration, kindness, compassion, and generosity to others?" The reason is, because everybody else seems to, and it's just that simple. Some show kindness to avoid embarrassment, to earn recognition, to relieve guilt, or because it hurts them to see other people hurting.

Remember the "Golden Rule" – "Do unto others as you would have them do unto you" – translates the general principle of caring and concern into an operational standard which encourages people to maximize the good and minimize the harm done to others.

Caring requires us to be as considerate, kind, compassionate, and generous as our duties and responsibilities will permit. But sometimes, even the love we want to share can be tough.

Sometimes, really caring requires us to make a difficult decision that may be considered unpleasant, but is a good decision in the long run. A decision you can be proud of.

"Guard well within yourself that treasure, <u>kindness</u>. Know how to give it without hesitation, how to lose without regret and how to acquire without meanness."
- – George Sand

– Caring Do's –
- Show you care about others through kindness, caring, generosity, and compassion.
- Live by the Golden Rule. Respect the dignity, privacy, and freedom of all individuals. Value and honor all people, no matter what they can do for you or to you. Respect others' property; take good care of property you are allowed to use, and don't' take or use property without permission. Respect

Character & Core Values!

****

the autonomy of others–tell them what they should know to make good choices about their own lives.

- Think how every decision, word, or action will impact every person involved.

- In terms of having concern for others, you should be compassionate and empathetic. You should be kind, loving, and considerate. Be thankful and express gratitude for what people do for you. Forgive others for their shortcomings.

- When you consider doing charity, be charitable and altruistic; give money, time, support, and comfort for the sake of making someone else's life better, not for praise or gratitude. Help people in need.

– Caring Don'ts –

- Don't be selfish.

- Don't be mean or cruel.

- Don't be insensitive to the feelings of others!

– <u>Fairness</u> –

As we consider the core value word fairness, we can see how it is just as important as the core value words responsibility, caring, trustworthiness, respect, and citizenship.

Fairness is one of the most difficult core values to define clearly. People often see those decisions that help them as fair and those decisions that do not as unfair.

Character & Core Values!

****

From an early age, you've probably had strong opinions about what is fair and what is not. This applies to everyone. One thing that is clear when it comes to fairness: it is often a matter of perception.

Although some decisions are clearly unfair, there is often more than one fair choice.

To ensure that choices are fair to as many people as possible, the rules of the decision-making process should be very clear to all involved and everyone should abide by the rules. Everyone must be treated the same under the rules.

– Fairness Do's –

- Treat people fairly.

- Listen to others and try to understand what they are feeling and saying.

- Consider all the facts, including opposing views, before making a decision.

- Make impartial decisions, using the same criteria, rules, or standards for everyone.

- Correct your mistakes.

- In terms of justice, you should be fair and just, treat people equally, and make decisions without favoritism or prejudice.

- In terms of openness, you should be open-minded and impartial. Consider what people have to say before you decide. Be careful and get the facts, including opposing viewpoints, before making decisions.

Character & Core Values!
****

- Don't take advantage of others' mistakes.

- Don't take more than your fair share.

- Don't let personal preferences, prejudices, or other feelings improperly interfere with decisions which should be based on merit.

– Trustworthiness –

As we consider the core value word trustworthiness, we can see how it is just as important as the core value words responsibility, caring, fairness, respect, and citizenship.

As you grow, you will find good people and people you can trust. You are honest, and you tell the truth. You are brave enough to do good things, even when people want you to do bad things.

You keep your promises; if you say you will do something, you do it. You say and do good things for your family and friends, and you are loyal.

– Honesty Do's –

- Say what you mean.
- Do the good things.

– Honesty Don'ts –

- Don't say you'll do something without really doing it.

Character & Core Values!

****

- Don't let anyone think something that isn't true.
- Don't tell a lie, steal, or cheat.

— Integrity Do's —

Integrity is not a conditional word. It doesn't blow in the wind or change with the weather. It is your inner image of yourself.

- Be brave and always do and say the right things.
- Do the right thing, even when people want you to do dishonest things.
- Be good team players all the time.
- Stand up for your beliefs. Follow your conscience. Be honorable and upright. Live by your principles, no matter what others say. Have the courage to do what is right and try new things even when it is hard. Build and guard your reputation.

— Integrity Don'ts —

- Don't do bad things, even when people try to force you.
- Don't do or say bad things, even if it means you'll lose friends, money, or anything else.

— Loyalty Do's —

- Help protect your family, friends, teachers, school, and community.
- Keep confidential information to yourself.

Character & Core Values!

****

– Loyalty Don'ts –

- Don't gossip or say things that hurt.
- Don't lie, cheat, or steal to get what you want.
- Don't ask anyone to do bad things.

– Respect –

As we consider the core value word respect, we can see how it is just as important as the core value words responsibility, caring, fairness, trustworthiness, and citizenship.

In our everyday lives, we all want a chance to be ourselves, make decisions, be accepted, and also be treated in a polite, decent way and have a little privacy.

Respectful people give others the information they need to make decisions about their lives.

Respectful people treat others with consideration. They do what is tasteful and proper in dealing with others. They don't stoop to such things as violence, meanness, or rudeness.

They tolerate other people's beliefs and accept individual differences without prejudice. They don't insist that everyone be like them.

Respectful people treat others as they want to be treated. They value others' beliefs. They help to build up others as they help them to value themselves.

Character & Core Values!

****

- Treat everyone with respect by being polite.

- Respect the individuality of others and be accepting of individual differences.

- Listen to others and try to understand their point of view.

- In terms of tolerance and acceptance, judge people on their merits, character, abilities and conduct. Not on their race, religion, nationality, age, sex, physical or mental condition, or socio-economical status.

-- Respect Don'ts --

- Respectful people do not insult, abuse, hurt, put down, mistreat, or harass others.

- Don't make unwanted comments about a person's appearance.

- Don't take advantage of other people.

- Don't hold back information people need to make decisions.

Character & Core Values!

****

– Citizenship –

As we consider the core value word citizenship, we can see how it is just as important as the core value words responsibility, caring, fairness, respect, and trustworthiness.

As a good citizen and neighbor, you should care about and pursue the common good. You can be a volunteer; help your school and community be better, cleaner, and safer. You can protect the environment by conserving resources and cleaning up after yourself. You can participate in making things better by voicing your opinion, voting, even serving on committees.

Core values are important because they help to develop all of the above attributes of great character that will help you make choices based on what is right.

It is not what we eat, but what we digest that makes us strong; it's not what we gain, but what we save that makes us rich; it's not what we read, but what we remember that makes us well-informed; and it's not what we profess, but what we practice that gives us integrity.

Your choices in life will complement the foundations that define you as an individual. Choose wisely.

"You can never do a kindness too soon, because you will never know how soon it will be too late."
- –Ralph Waldo Emerson

"Mistakes are a fact of life. It is the response to error that count."
- – Nikki Giovanni

Character & Core Values!

★★

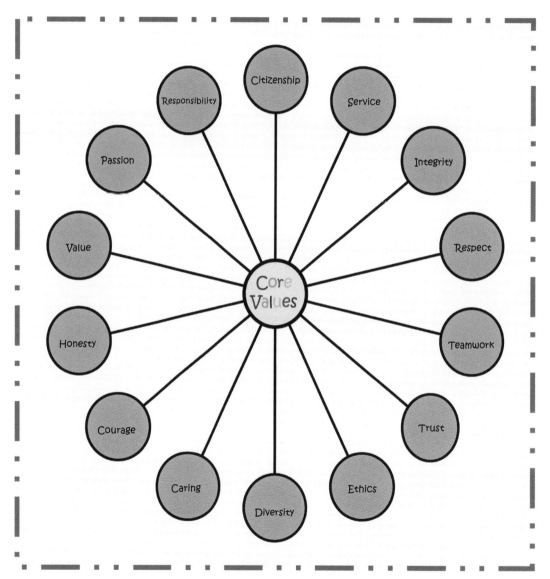

From the inner circle to the outer circles, your character really counts in the choices you make.

Character & Core Values!

****

Your core values can grow like blossoming flowers, when you aspire in life and not be afraid to define who you are as an individual. Someday, you will be able to share your journey and be an inspiration!

Service   Honesty   Courage
Integrity   **Trust**   **Patience**
Respect   Value
Teamwork   **Caring**   **Passion**
Diligence   Fairness   Diversity
Citizenship   **Empathy**
Perseverance   Responsibility   Ethic
Self-Control   **Self-Esteem**
Trustworthiness   Patience

Regardless of what labels we put on our values, each of us must discover what they mean to us personally, and we must live by them in order to benefit from them.

The connection between character and core values will help you to develop a passion for listening, sharing, caring, and understanding.

As you make this transformation, you will be able to make changes happen in your life little by little.

Chapter 2

Character & Core Values!

★★

The Eight Strengths of Character outlined in the following chart are important because they focus on you as an individual. The Eight Strengths focus on the following:

(1) The assets a person needs for success–for a productive, ethical, and fulfilling life in school and beyond.

(2) How your individuality and strengths, such as being a community leader and great citizen, are important.

(3) Moral character, which enables you to treat others with respect and care, and ensures that you use ethical means to achieve your performance goals.

(4) How your passion for life-long learning is important.

(5) Performance character, which is needed to realize your potential for excellence.

(6) How your ethical behavior will help in defining who you are.

This charted path of influence is what you live by from day to day.

Character & Core Values!

****

Eight Strengths of Character

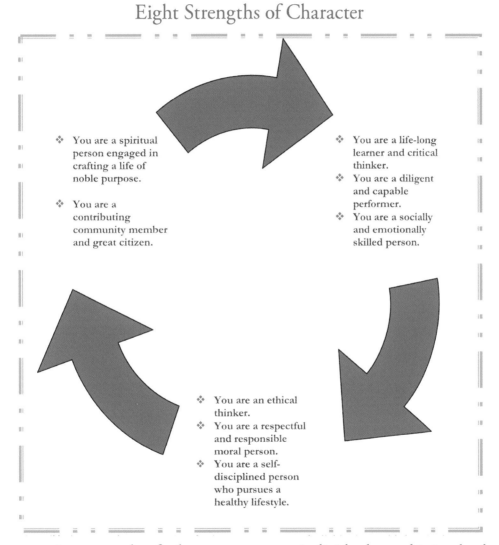

❖ You are a spiritual person engaged in crafting a life of noble purpose.

❖ You are a contributing community member and great citizen.

❖ You are a life-long learner and critical thinker.

❖ You are a diligent and capable performer.

❖ You are a socially and emotionally skilled person.

❖ You are an ethical thinker.

❖ You are a respectful and responsible moral person.

❖ You are a self-disciplined person who pursues a healthy lifestyle.

Your life is a continuous cycle of who you are as an individual, combining both moral and performance character.

Character & Core Values!

****

From reading the previous sections, you should have an understanding that character and core values are really important in setting the stage for life-long dreams.

We can see why the Six C's of Character, the Virtues, and the Eight Strengths of Character, are important assets to your character, and aligned with your core values, help define who you are as GALS!™.

As you dare to dream show passion and be compassionate, believe in your dreams.

Your dreams, as you continue on your journey are about hope and beating the odds, while you tap into your feelings of pride and passion.

Anything is attainable as long as you have the courage to dare to believe and continue to dare to dream.

As GALS!™ when you dare to believe, the impossible becomes the possible.

"I have learned over the years that when one's mind is made up, this diminishes fear; knowing what must be done does away with fear."

- – Rosa Parks, civil rights leader (1913 – 2005)

Character & Core Values!

★★★

"Values guide our behavior, determines the work we choose, and establish priorities for how we use our time."

"Living our values ignites pride in who we are and provides us with dignity and gives us energy for life."

"An honest assessment of our strengths and limitations, grounds us in reality, allowing us to act in ways that are self-aware."

- – Carol Anderson and Patricia Shafer, "Enlightened Power", Reprinted with permission of John Wiley & Sons, Inc. Copyright © 2005. All rights reserved.

Dare to Believe!

****

GALS!™, sometimes life requires a leap of faith while at the same time it provides the light for your journey!

When you believe in something, you accept it as being true, real, or genuine, and you have a clear understanding of what it is. In this chapter, I present to you more maxims, paraphrases, and words of encouragement to help you follow your passion in life and believe.

GALS!™, that believe in themselves have the power and authority to control their destiny.

"Real change begins with understanding what you believe."

"Out of awareness comes the ability to inform how you act in the world. The framework for what you believe on a personal level sets the stage for everything you do."

- – Rayona Sharpnack, "Enlightened Power". Reprinted with permission of John Wiley & Sons, Inc. Copyright © 2005. All rights reserved.

- Let go of the place that holds you.
  - o Let go of the place that flinches.
  - o Let go of the place that controls.
  - o Let go of the place that you fear.
  - o Just let the ground support you.

"GALS!™"........Believe in You!

Dare to Believe!

****

Do it with grace, ease, and enjoyment. Take in the moment, then relax, rejuvenate, and meditate. Through your own realization, you will enjoy what you are doing.

"Do not curse the darkness. Instead, light a candle! Let your **dreams** light the way on your journey."

> • – Gandhi

"One does not become enlightened by imagining figures of light, but by making the darkness conscious."

> • – Carl Jung

"You have to leave the city of your comfort and go into the wilderness of your intuition. What you will discover will be wonderful. What you will discover will be yourself."

> • – Alan Alda

"It's not that today is the first day of your rest of your life, but that now is all there is of my life."

> • – Hugh Prather

"Do not follow where the path may lead. Go ahead where there is not a path and leave a trail."

> • – Ralph Waldo Emerson

"Even if you are on the right track, you will get run over if you just sit there."

> • – Will Rogers

31

Dare to Believe!

✶✶

"The only way to discover the limits of the possible is to go beyond them into the impossible."

> • – Unknown

"There are two kinds of people in the world. Those who walk into a room and say, "There you are" and those who say, "Here I am."

> • – Abigail Van Buren

"Let yourself be silently drawn by the strange pull of what you really love. It will not lead you astray."

> • – Rumi

"Don't be afraid your life will end. Be afraid that it will never begin."

> • – Grace Hansen

"Risk everything. Care no more for others' opinions, for those voices, do the hardest thing on earth for you. Act for yourself."

> • – Katherine Mansfield

"Remember, if people talk behind your back, it only means you are two steps ahead."

> • – Fannie Flagg

"Fear is that little darkroom where negatives are developed."

> • – Michael Pritchard

"The time is always right to do what is right."

> • – Dr. Martin Luther King, Jr.

Dare to Believe!

****

"Having a voice is so important in defining who you are."

• – Christine Brumfield

"Life is not without its many challenges; believe that you are in charge of your destiny."

• – Christine Brumfield

"If everything is an awakening, you will never grow old. You will just keep growing."

• – Gail Sheehy

Humans, not miracles of magic, bring about change.

• – Unknown

"Perseverance is a great element of success. If you only knock long enough and loud enough at the gate, you are sure to wake up somebody."

• – Henry Wadsworth Longfellow

Change is the scariest thing in the world – but it means understanding that sometimes you must believe you have to be flexible.

GALS!™, shall rise to the occasion of every challenge in life, believe in yourself and **dream** big.

GALS!™, always be a first–rate version of yourself, instead of a second–rate version of somebody else. Believe in yourself.

Dare to Believe!

****

"Yesterday is history, tomorrow is a mystery, and today is a gift; that's why they call it the present."

- • – Unknown

GALS!™, believe that you can create your own reality!

Good ideas are not enough; you must follow through with a plan. A good leader will plan the work and then work the plan all the way through to the end to achieve the desired results.

GALS!™, as you move forward in life, remember that, like in a chess game, the person who thinks the furthest ahead has the most control over the outcome.

"Others will not value what you have until you do."

- • – Michael Josephson, president and founder, Character Counts Coalition and Josephson Institute of Ethics

"Discoveries are often made by not following instructions, but by going off the main road, and trying the untried."

- • – Frank Tyger, Forbes

The only way to enjoy anything in this life is to earn it first.

"Other people's opinion of you does not have to become your reality."

- • – Les Brown, entrepreneur, motivational speaker and author

Dare to Believe!

****

"Doing the best at this moment puts you in the best place for the next moment."

- – Oprah Winfrey,
    talk show host, author,
    entrepreneur, actress,
    and beautiful lady

GALS!™, believing strongly in your **dreams** can effect your **emotions** -- how you feel.

Emotions focus on how you feel about a situation. They are a part of who you are as an individual, and you should not feel ashamed of feeling a certain way.

Expressing your feelings and your **emotions** is perfectly normal. You are allowing your **emotions** to balance out with the core values and as a result, you allow your beliefs and **dreams** to become a reality.

As you try to keep your **emotions** under control and yourself together, embracing them is not hard, simply because our **emotions** are a form of personal expression. You must let go of the place that holds you and begin to take control of your life and **emotions**.

Emotions!

****

GALS!™, what do you think about – when you think about your own emotions?

This chapter will help you to understand how your emotions affect you on a daily basis and how you can use them wisely.

Emotions can simply be defined as how you feel about yourself, a particular situation, your friends, your school, your parents, and your teachers to name a few areas.

Emotions relate to your behavior and the feelings you have about love, happiness, sadness, being surprised, joy, fear and even pain. We use our emotions daily. Let's discover how to deal with our emotions.

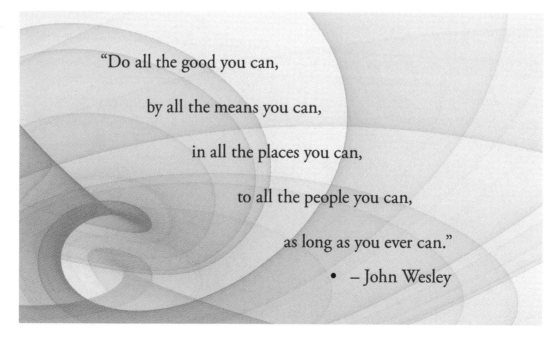

"Do all the good you can,

by all the means you can,

in all the places you can,

to all the people you can,

as long as you ever can."

• – John Wesley

Emotions!

****

Emotions are defined as the extent to which a person is attuned to his or her feelings and to the feelings of others.

It includes several interrelated components and skills. An aspect of emotions called "Emotional Intelligence" deals with two concepts that require you to look at both self-awareness and communication skills. These are very important skills to have for everyday living.

Combined, the two concepts can provide you with the ability to accurately express your feelings to others.

Emotions can help leaders solve complex problems, make better decisions, plan how to use their time effectively, adapt their behavior to the situation, and manage crisis. Emotions are relevant for leadership effectiveness in many ways.

GALS!™, in order for you to be able to evaluate or understand the concept of emotional intelligence, you must first understand the key competencies. These competencies will help you to understand how to deal with your daily actions and responses to circumstances.

The key competencies for emotional leadership are described in the following four domains. Two of the four domains are directed as looking at ourselves and evaluating your internal competencies. The other two domains are directed at focusing on others.

The four domains are self-awareness, self-management, social awareness and relationship awareness.

Emotions!

****

According to Dr. Daniel Goleman, Emotional Intelligence (Mayer & Salvoey, 1995)," effective leadership requires the four domains to work in concert."

GALS!.. as you consider the four domains outlined below, think about how your life could be affected when your emotions become a part of your everyday decisions.

The first domain is self–awareness and includes an awareness of your beliefs and how you express your emotions.

When you are in touch with how you are reacting and know the core values you want to use to help guide your actions, you are in, what is called an awareness of self.

In this domain, you also have the ability to accurately do a self-assessment. This means you can apply an understanding of your strengths and weaknesses and you are willing to listen and act on constructive feedback.

You also have a sense of self-confidence, which is having a firm belief in the strengths that will allow you to challenge yourself and not be afraid to take risks.

So we can say that, self–awareness is having an understanding of our own moods and emotions, knowing how they evolve, how they can change over time and their implications for task performance. Also self-awareness can help you reflect on how your emotions can play a vital part in interpersonal relationships.

Self–awareness makes it easier to understand your own needs and likely reactions if certain events occurred, thereby facilitating evaluations for alternative solutions.

Emotions!

★★

The second domain is self–management and include areas that will help you to manage yourself while in many situations.

In this domain, you want to have the ability to manage your self-control and those emotions that might hinder effective actions.   You can do this by adapting to your environment.

Being able to adapt to new realities and being flexible in your thinking, is a form of managing your self-control.

When you think of self-management, you should also think about personal achievement, the dreams and goals you might have. Achievement can be described as having a desire to reach high standards and to continually learn, improve, lead, and inspire.

Another great self-management tool is having great initiative, that includes finding and making opportunities rather than waiting passively for opportunities to come to you. This involves taking on risks and following through with challenges that may arise and seeking help when needed.

Last, but not least, being an optimistic person, is good. Optimism is expecting the best and seeing change as an opportunity. Believe that you are the best, and think positively.

"Optimism is the faith that leads to achievement. Nothing can be done without hope and confidence."

> • – Helen Keller

The last two domains will focus on how your emotions can have an affect on others.

Emotions!

****

The third domain is social-awareness and include areas that can help you deal with others in many social situations.

One area that is important for you to understand emotionally is empathy. Empathy is being able to accurately pick up on how others are seeing their particular situation and how they are feeling about it. You can have emotions that can be shared with others while understanding those around you.

Within this domain called social-awarencss, the concept of organizational awareness is important for you to understand because it provides the ability for you to be able to notice and understand the political dynamics in groups and organizations.

Social groups or organizations can include being in a part for a school play, participating in a sport you like, or even running for an elected board position, and how you can adjust yourself in each situation.

While keeping the concept of social-awareness in mind, you can be a wonderful inspiration to those around you.

Your influence and special attention to how well friends, and family, your schoolmates, or teammates are being satisfied can play a big part into how well you engage and interact with people and how you are able to get their buy-in.

When you spend time showing a genuine interest in helping others to grow and reach their goals, this shows your maturity and growth as well. It really doesn't matter if the goals are personal or part of a team effort, you play a special part.

Emotions!

✗✗✗

The fourth domain is called relationship-management and includes areas that can help you in a team environment.

In recognizing and championing change in a way that can help you to overcome barriers, being a change catalyst will allow all those involved to feel comfortable in any environment. It is an awareness of reaching out to everyone and treating them all the same.

Feeling comfortable enough with a certain conflict to talk about it and then being able to provide constructive directions and feedback to the situation, you are handling conflict management in a way that is beneficial to all those involved and provides maturity and growth for all GALs!™.

Creating an environment whether it's at home, school, or on the playground, in which people seek to work together and commit to joint goals is teamwork and collaboration. You will use this concept throughout life.

Always be kind to your friends, because friendship is like a bank account, you can't continue to draw on it without making deposits. The smallest good deed is better than the grandest good intentions.

GALs!™, understanding your emotions are so important that I hope you read this chapter over and over to really gain an understanding of what matters most. Afterwards you should be able to feel confident to put together a strategy to effectively express your emotions in a way that will benefit you in your everyday lives.

Do not be afraid to express your feelings no matter how different they are to others.

Chapter 4

Emotions!

****

When you combine all of the previous chapters up this now, i.e., dreaming, believing, character and core values, you should envision yourself in a place where your level of understanding of each chapter has helped you to feel good about who you are and how you should treat others.

You are someone that others want to be and now in a position where they are inspired just by who you are.

"While we are free to choose our actions, we are not free to choose the consequences of our actions."

- – Stephen Covey

Leadership!

✶✶✶

GALS!™, what do you think about -- when you think about Leadership?

This chapter will help you to learn more about being a leader. It will help you to understand what it takes to be a great leader and the qualities needed. After reading this chapter, you will understand that leadership is one of your greatest strengths.

Leadership is about inspiring others to follow, not because you are likable or have a lot of friends, but because of your strong belief in yourself and the ability to inspire others to want to follow you.

As you go through life, you will hear the following question asked many times: "Are leaders born or made?"

Leadership is not a place, it's not a gene, and it's not a secret code that can't be deciphered by ordinary people.

The truth is, leadership is an observable set of skills and abilities. In which, any skill can be strengthened, embraced, and enhanced, given the motivation, desire, practice, feedback, role models, and coaching available to each of you.

Effective leadership creates an environment that will significantly change the dynamics of many circumstances.

It defines a future that is aligned with a vision that inspires you as an individual to make it happen despite any road blocks that may come your way.

Leadership!

✱✱✱

"The supreme quality for leadership is unquestionably integrity. Without it, no real success is possible, no matter whether it is, in a football field, in an army, or in an office."

• – Dwight D. Eisenhower

Leadership is based on your emotions and definitely has an effect on your character, the virtues, and the core values that define who you are as an individual.

Out of awareness comes the ability to inform how you act in the world. The very framework for what you believe on a personal level sets the stage for everything else.

By following your passion, you can do anything and be anybody. Following your passion in life is the energy that makes you unique as well as special. Your passion comes from within your soul; you feel it straight from your heart.

As a great leader, you don't spend time on negative situations or negative people. Leaders are able to redirect their energy forward and are able to generate positive results. Real change, for leaders, begins with understanding what you believe.

If you do something different that has more influence, more visibility and a lot more opportunity, you are able to build relationships with other dynamic GALS!™.

As a leader, you have the strength and courage to move away from your comfort zone.

The challenge for every leader lies in reaching within our own self-consciousness and finding that source of hope.

Leadership!

★★

Within all of us lies the mere power to evoke and articulate one's personal ideal self-image and the shared ideas that flow from it.

This kind of leadership requires not only a vision, but a clear picture of the reality you are facing.

It is fortunate then, that your emotions can be understood. The process is not easy. It takes time, and most of all, patience and a sincere, heartfelt commitment to endure the life–changing strategies that comes with change.

Leadership is not about commanding and controlling a particular situation, a group event, or even a friend, but the powerful art of persuading people to work toward a common goal.

Remember to dare to dream, lead, and inspire.

People change when they are emotionally engaged and committed. Change is the scariest thing in the world, but it means understanding that sometimes you have to be flexible. Humans, not miracles of magic, bring about change.

"We need a new vision, a new definition of power and leadership. We must move toward a model of creative cooperation. There is a need in the world for women to come together and imagine, define, and lead us toward a sane and sustainable culture."

- – Dr. Johnnetta Cole, president of Bennett College for Women. Spoken at the Women in Power Conference, Omega Institute, September 11, 2004.

Leadership!

****

GALS!™ as you grow, you become natural resources optimizers, able to access energy and ideas that may be left untapped by a traditional perspective.

"Being passion-powered and vision-guided are two essential elements required for exceptional human performance, but without action, you are just a vivid dreamer."

"What we envision and hold dear must have a way to come into being. Effective daily action requires a strategy and feedback to let us know if we are on the right track. Most of all, we create daily mental and physical practices that keep the vision alive and our actions aligned as we move closer to our goal each day."

"Passion and vision without actions get you nowhere. Passion and vision without a plan or effective daily practice make you a dreamer."

"Most people have experienced a time when all three elements have fallen into place, often by accident. The role of a leader is to align those elements by design."

- – Marilyn King, Enlightened Power. Reprinted with permission of John Wiley & Sons, Inc. Copyright © 2005. All rights reserved.

"Where there is no vision – there is no hope."
- – George Washington Carver

GALS!™, as great leaders, you want to have an inner circle reaching outward in every direction, a circle of influence.

Leadership!

****

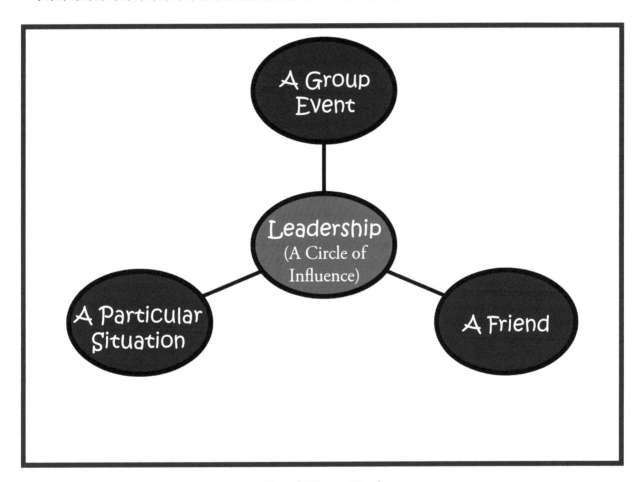

Find Your Path
Share Your Journey!

From your Inner Circle of Influence
Inspire Others…..!!

Leadership!

****

What GALS!™ Know and Will Do!

Leadership is based on an individual's performance, ability, effectiveness, and action. So when you help others, you are ultimately helping yourself become an "Inspiration."

"L" GALS!™ will Leap into their dreams.

"E" GALS!™ will follow their own Energy.

"A" GALS!™ will Allow others to mentor them, and they in turn will mentor others.

"D" GALS!™ know that Decisions are many and will always follow their hearts, knowing their character will ultimately define who they are.

"E" GALS!™ know that Ethics are important and, as leaders, will always take the high road.

"R" GALS!™ know that Responsibility is theirs to behold and will accept it with dignity and grace.

"S" GALS!™ will Share their experiences and ideas.

"As a leader...the challenge is to be a light, not a judge; to be a model, not a critic."
- – Stephen Covey on Leadership

Leadership!

★★★

Girls As Leaders! -- GALS! will succeed as leaders when they are a living examples of their core values and character.

"L"   GALS! love being inspirational Leaders.

"E"   GALS! are Ethical.

"A"   GALS! are Admirable.

"D"   GALS! are Diligent.

"E"   GALS! are Excellent individuals.

"R"   GALS! are Respectful.

"S"   GALS! have great Self-esteem.

The best leaders draw on moral qualities to influence others through inspiration, persuasion, trust, and loyalty.

"The fragrance always stays in the hand that gives the rose."
 • – Hada Bejar

Leadership!

****

Girls As Leaders! – GALS! will succeed as leaders when they have fun believing and will "Dare to Dream."

"L"   GALS! Love living their dreams.

"E"   GALS! are Exceptional individuals.

"A"   GALS! are Aspiring.

"D"   GALS! are Driven to do their best.

"E"   GALS! are Enthusiastic about life.

"R"   GALS! are Responsible individuals.

"S"   GALS! enjoy Sharing their journey in life.

"You gain strength, courage, and confidence by every experience in which you really stop to look fear in the face. You must do the thing which you think you cannot do."

•   – Eleanor Roosevelt

Chapter 5

Leadership!

****

Leadership guidance can be defined in the eight laws of leadership. The laws are as follows:

- "First, maintain absolute integrity.
- Second, know your stuff.
- Third, declare your expectations.
- Fourth, show uncommon commitment.
- Fifth, expect positive results.
- Sixth, take care of your family and friends.
- Seventh, put duty before self.
- And finally, eighth, get out in front."
    - – Former Air Force General William Cohen

The laws embrace important competencies like knowledge, communication skills, commitment, optimism, caring and a powerful sense of duty.

The foundation of a successful leader is based on an individual's character, which include values such as honor, trustworthiness, and courage.

The "Eight Universal Laws of Leadership" by General William A. Cohen were used by Michael Josephson in his Free Weekly Commentary E-Newsletter #429.1 (Sept. 20 - 29 2005). Reprinted with permission of the Josephson Institute of Ethics, ©2006 www.charactercounts.org. All rights reserved.

Chapter 5

Leadership!

✸✸

The best leaders draw on moral qualities which are a vital part of the basic foundation of core values and a part of our character. The moral qualities serve as a guide that influences others through inspiration, persuasion, trust, and loyalty.

Much has been written about women not supporting other women across age, racial lines, culture, and status. The barriers cannot be dissolved without making time to reflect on our differences and to create, as social commentators call it, "an irresistible fusion" across gender, age, race, and ethnicity. This fusion is also critically needed in a world where we see few examples of reflective leadership.

- – Anna Deavere Smith, actress

"We don't find ourselves in a blinding flash of insight, nor do we change overnight. We learn by doing, and each experience is part answer and part question."

"Whatever the first step, the process gradually changes the nature of what we know and what we seek to learn. Transformation happens less by grand design or careful strategy than by the ongoing experiments that enhance our capacity to become the myriad possibilities that define us."

- – Herminia Ibarra, Enlightened Power. Reprinted with permission of John Wiley & Sons, Inc. Copyright © 2005. All rights reserved.

GALS!™ as you "Dare to Dream" and embrace your character, core values, and the virtues, you now have the confidence to "Dare to Believe" in yourself, and not be afraid to share as well as show your emotions.

Leadership!

✶✶✶

Inspire others to follow your lead and do the right thing, despite the costs and risks. You do this not because it will yield approval or some advantage, but simply because it is the right thing to do. You turn the impossible into the possible.

In today's cynical times, it's easy to think that such leadership is unattainable; yet in every walk of life, hundreds of young men and women, as well as parents, teachers, coaches, and civic activists, fit the standard mold.

What's more, each one of you could be among them.

But you have something special: you have an understanding of who you are. You have character.

Trust yourself. Think for yourself. Act for yourself. Speak for yourself. Be yourself.
- – Marva Collin
  African-American educator

Life is too short to belittle. Make the best of yours. "If you want to be successful, don't give or take excuses."
- – Florence Nightingale

In the quest to truly understand who we are, our beliefs, values, needs, emotions, character, and core values, we must make our hearts sing.

Leadership!

****

GALs!™ – Step Into the Limelight

– Stand tall and imagine a string attached to the body like a puppet's, pulling the head and the spine into alignment.

– Get rid of the all-too-common tilted head that throws stance and directions slightly off-course.

– Maintain direct eye contact and avoid dropping your gaze to the floor.

– Stop using self-deprecating remarks when stating your credentials and stature.

– Step into the light and show your real stuff: intelligence, authority, accomplishments, power, and personality.

- –Peggy Klaus, Enlightened Power. Reprinted with permission of John Wiley & Sons, Inc. Copyright © 2005. All rights reserved.

Inspire!   Be Good!   Have fun!   Believe!

Leadership!

****

Bring your Dreams to Life!

&

Share your Journey!

"Fame is a vapor, popularity an accident; riches take wing; only your character endures."

• – Horace Greeley

Success Is Yours!

****

Ralph Waldo Emerson defined success as "To laugh often and much; to win the respect of intelligent people and the affection of children; to appreciate beauty; to find the best in others; to leave the world a little better; whether by a healthy child or a garden patch; …to know even one life has breathed easier because you have lived. This is success."

The primary goal of this book is to provide an effective resource to help GALs! ™ – Girls As Leaders! ™ achieve their goals in life while building their character and **leadership** skills along the way.

The unprecedented challenges faced by our world today are not caused by a need for more laws, better education, or wealthier citizens, but a need for great character.

The issue upon which national success revolves is the personal character of a nation's people. The character of a nation can only be strengthened one person at a time.

As you "Dare to Dream" you open the world to your beliefs, thinking about the impossible and daring to make it the possible. "The struggle to strengthen our national character is the most important struggle in which we must engage."

- – Anthony Harrigan

Achieving success involves a combination of skills, insight, and discipline. Achieving greatness requires this combination and also the ability to inspire yourself and others to a sense of purpose, vision, and direction.

Success Is Yours!

****

While each of us has the tools, the question is, how do we unlock them to lead beyond the ordinary into greatness?

"Success is going from failure to failure without loss of enthusiasm."
- — Sir Winston Churchill

We must learn the process of how to speak our minds and encourage others to engage in meaningful dialogue, discover how to build, strengthen, and lead others by leveraging individual skills; and learn how to anticipate strategies and trends, rather than react to them.

We must build true success in our lives and work.

"You are in charge of your own attitude, whatever others do or circumstances you face. The only person you can control is yourself. Worry more about your attitude than your aptitude or lineage."
- — Marian Wright Edelman in The Measure of Our Success

Being successful doesn't depend on what you have or what you do, your chances of a successful life depends on who you are as an individual and how well you know yourself.

Success is different for everyone. For example, you might think of yourself as successful, yet in the eyes of someone else, you may not be. Don't let this distract you. The very fact that we are all different means that every path to a successful life will be different as well.

When you dare to believe you can be more powerful and talented than you could ever imagine. You must spend time discovering your strengths, eliminating your weaknesses and focusing

Success Is Yours!

****

on what you really want from your life.   Commit to begin building your successful future by **daring to dream**.

"GALS!™" .... !!!!!

"We cannot hold a torch to light another's path without brightening our own."
- • - Ben Sweetland, author

Dream Big!

Believe the Impossible!

Inspire Others!

Lead with your Heart!

"Dare To Dream"

****

Dynamic, inspiring words from a song entitled "**Dare To Dream**" by Onaje Allan Gumbs /Charles Allen – Onaje Music/ASCAP)/Origin Music (BMI).

- "Daylight is breaking through all the clouds we've seen together
- More storms are bound to come
  - o We can't harbor here forever
- Our wings were made for the sky
  - o No matter what, we must fly
- Stand up and **DARE TO DREAM** of higher mountains for you and me
  - o No matter how hard it seems
    - DARE TO DREAM
- We're gonna reach the stars
  - o Despite all the winds against us
  - o They say we can't go that far
  - o But I know we got it in us
- Our wings were made for the sky
  - o No matter what, we must fly
- Stand up and **DARE TO DREAM** of higher mountains for you and me
  - o No matter how hard it seems
    - DARE TO DREAM
- And if we do fall, we'll fight through it all
  - o We'll stand like heroes of a brave new dawn

59

- Our wings were made for the sky
  - o   No matter what, we must fly
- Stand up and **DARE TO DREAM** of higher mountains for you and me
  - o   No matter how hard it seems
- STAND up ----- STAND up! and
  - ■ "DARE TO DREAM"

Definitions
Character & Core Values
****

Caring –

Deals with the essence of being a caring person, doing caring things, and encouraging young people to treat others with kindness, concern, and generosity. Be kind • Be compassionate and show you care • Express gratitude • Forgive others • Help people in need.

Character –

Deals with the set of qualities that make somebody or something distinctive, especially somebody's qualities of mind, feelings, personality, or appearance. "Good character is understanding, caring, and acting on core ethical values like honesty, responsibility, and caring for others. It means knowing the good, loving the good, and doing good."

• –Professor Kevin Ryan

Citizenship –

Deals with what makes people good citizens and how one good citizen can make an important difference to the community, i.e. volunteering / mentoring. Do your share to make your school and community better • Cooperate • Get involved in community affairs • Stay informed • Vote • Be a good neighbor • Obey laws and rules • Respect authority • Protect the environment.

Courage –

Deals with what it means to be morally courageous, especially in the face of negative peer pressure, and how that empowers your life.

Definitions

Character & Core Values

****

Diligence –   Deals with how we benefit from being persistent in any hard-working task and how we should approach each important task with discipline and focus while always doing our best.

Diversity –   Deals with accepting an overall variety of differences, as well as socioeconomic and gender differences, in a group, society, or institution. Accepting cultural differences from what is considered normal or expected.

Ethics –   "Deals with how moral standards affect our conduct and how those moral standards govern the appropriate conduct for an individual or group."
- – Albert Schweitzer

Fairness –   Deals with what it takes to be fair and just and how much our personal actions affect other people. Play by the rules • Take turns and share • Be open-minded • Listen to others • Don't take advantage of others • Don't blame others carelessly.

Fun –   Deals with enjoying life and all it has to offer, daring to dream and reaching for the stars. Know that the sky is the limit. Dream big.

Honesty –   Deals with how choosing to be honest or dishonest profoundly affects our character and relationships with others.

Definitions
Character & Core Values
****

Integrity –   Deals with the quality of possessing and steadfastly adhering to high moral principles or professional standards. Integrity is a gift to you as well as to the world.

Passion –   Deals with having strong emotions involving a subject or activity.

Patience –   Deals with a willingness to wait and endure without complaint.

Perseverance –   Deals with staying with a task and not giving up.

Respect –   Deals with having respectful behavior which helps to create a climate of civility. Respecting others shows great consideration or thoughtfulness. Respect also deals with showing regard for self, others, property, and those in authority. You should treat others with respect • Follow the Golden Rule • Be tolerant of differences • Use good manners, not bad language • Be considerate of the feelings of others • Don't threaten, hit or hurt anyone • Finally, deal peacefully with anger, insults, and disagreements.

Responsibility –   Deals with how taking responsibility can put you in charge of your life and strengthen your personal relationship with others. It also shows a willingness to be accountable for your actions and choices without blaming others. Do what you are supposed to do • Persevere--keep on trying! • Always do your best • Use self-control • Be self-disciplined • Think before you act, and consider the consequences.

Definitions

Character & Core Values

****

Self-control –   Deals with managing your behavior in a positive way.

Self-esteem –   Deals with having and demonstrating a positive belief in you.

Service –   Deals with extending time and effort to others.

Teamwork –   Deals with a cooperative effort between a number of individuals. It is the act of working together to achieve a common aim and doing what is asked or required.

Trustworthiness –   Deals with being able to be trusted by others to be counted on. You should be honest and not deceive, cheat, or steal • You should be reliable, do what you say you'll do, and have the courage to do the right thing • Build a good reputation • Be loyal – stand by your family, friends, and country.

Value –   Deals with accepting the principles or standards of an individual or a group.

```
*****************************************
```
Grateful Acknowledgements
```
*****************************************
```

Is for permission to reprint the following:
Lyrics reprinted with permission granted by Onaje Allan Gumbs, from the CD titled "DARE to DREAM" by Onaje Allan Gumbs /Charles Allen – Onaje Music/(ASCAP)/Origin Music (BMI). All rights reserved.

To learn more about Onaje and his music, please visit his website at: www.onajeallangumbs.com

```
**********************************
```
About the Illustrator & Book Cover Design
```
**********************************
```

Elaine A. Young, Designer/Art Director of Hopscotch Communications. To learn more about her work, please visit www.hopscotchcommunications.com

Cathi Stevenson, Book Cover Designer and President of Book Cover Express. To learn more about her work, please visit www.bookcoverdesign.com

****

Additional Resources

****

To learn more about CHARACTER COUNTS!_{SM} and related services and products, please visit the following websites www.charactercounts.org and www.josephsoninstituteofethics.org. Reprint permission. All rights reserved.

To learn more about the CHARACTER COUNTS!_{SM} Commentaries by Michael Josephson, please visit and subscribe to www.commentary@jethics.org. Reprint permission. All rights reserved.

To learn more about The Eight Strengths of Character by Thomas Lickona and Matthew Davidson, please read "Smart & Good Schools: Integrating Excellence and Ethics for Success in School, Work, and Beyond, Cortland, N.Y. Center for the 4th and 5th Rs (Respect & Responsibility)/Washington, D.C. Character Education Partnership. Reprint permission for educational purposes. All rights reserved. Copyright © (2005).

To learn more about Emotional Intelligence by Dr. Daniel Goleman, please read: Leadership in Organizations, by Dr. Daniel Goleman, (Mayer & Salvoey, 1995). All rights reserved.

Enlightened Power - How Women Are Transforming The Practice of Leadership. Copyright © 2005 by Linkage Inc. John Wiley & Sons, Inc. Editors Linda Coughlin, Ellen Wingard and Keith Hollihan. Reprint permission. All rights reserved.

The Stuff of Heroes: The Eight Universal Laws of Leadership, by General William A. Cohen. CHARACTER COUNTS!_{SM} Commentaries. Please visit and subscribe to: www. commentary@jethics.org. Reprint permission. All rights reserved.

About the Author

****

Christine "Kris" Brumfield has a passion for wanting girls to reach for the stars and follow their dreams. After being diagnosed with cancer and now as a cancer survivor, she has realized that life really is too short to put things off and reminds her-self of what matters most. So she finished this book.

She has always been a mentor for young girls through her involvement in community relations, whether it's with the Society of Women Engineers, the Girls Scouts of America, or Boys and Girls Clubs.

Printed in the United States
87835LV00002B